This Starfish Bay book belongs to

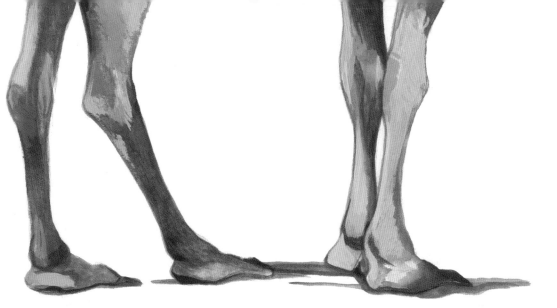

Whose Toes Do You Suppose?

Written by Richard Turner
Illustrated by Margaret Tolland

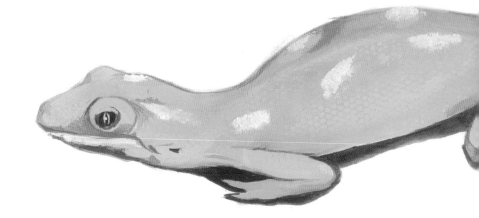

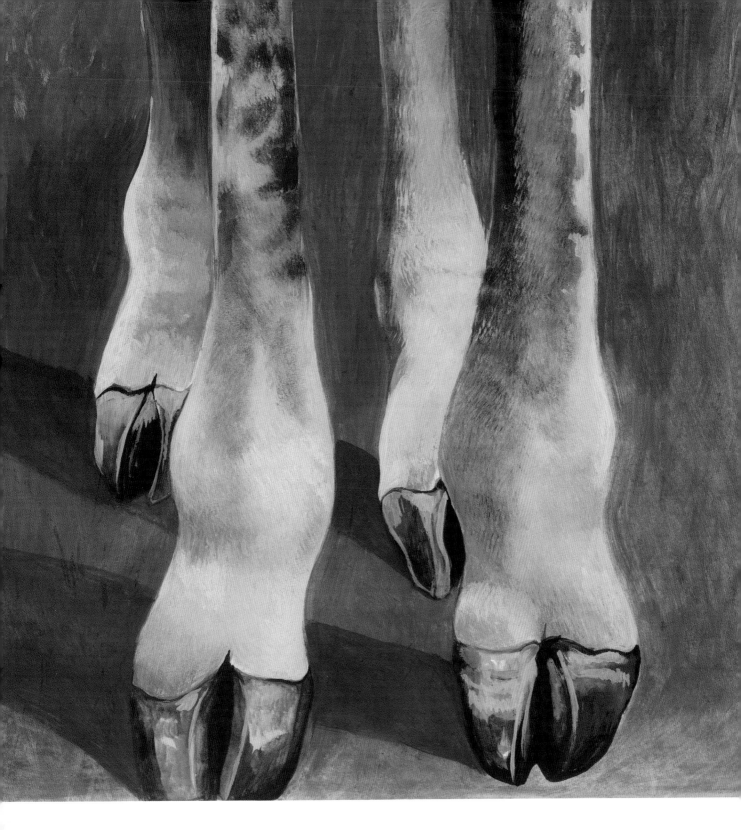

Whose toes do you suppose?

Giraffe

Hooves with toes and legs rising high,
so tall it appears to touch the sky.
An elegant animal with a gentle lope,
cloaked in a spotty overcoat.
Hiding in shadows when danger's near,
and a tongue so long it can lick its ears.

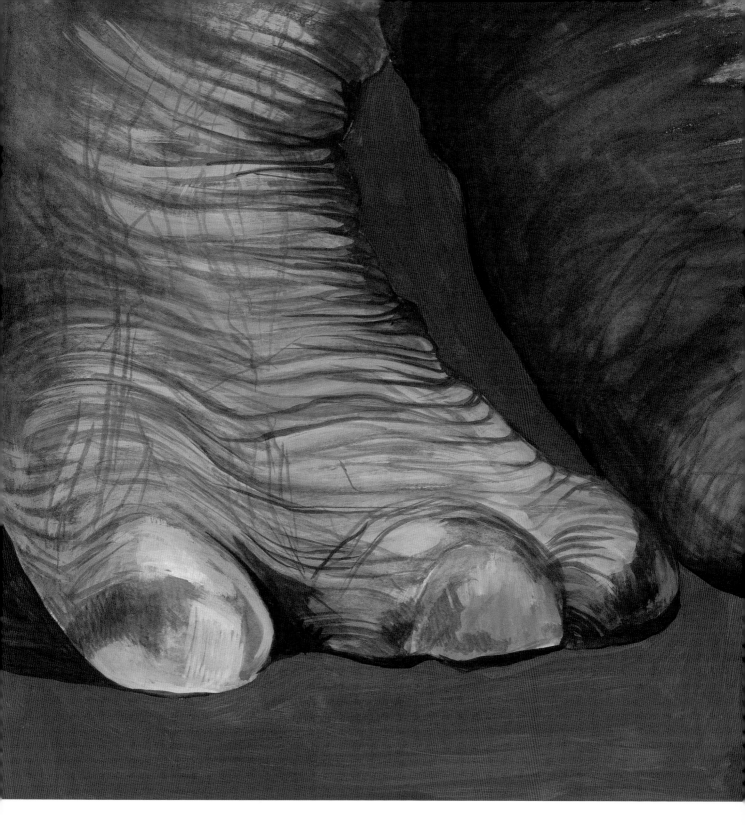

Whose toes do you suppose?

Hippopotamus

Each of these feet has four webbed toes.
When diving, their ears and nostrils close.
In water is where they spend most of the day.
During the night they come out to graze.
They have short, stumpy legs with a body so plump
and a reputation for being a grump.

Whose toes do you suppose?

Penguin

Three toes with claws stop the slipping and sliding
as they waddle on ice when not swimming and diving.
With flippers, not wings, this bird cannot fly,
but In icy waters they are incredibly spry.
They swim with grace and lightning speed
and can sleep while standing. How strange indeed.

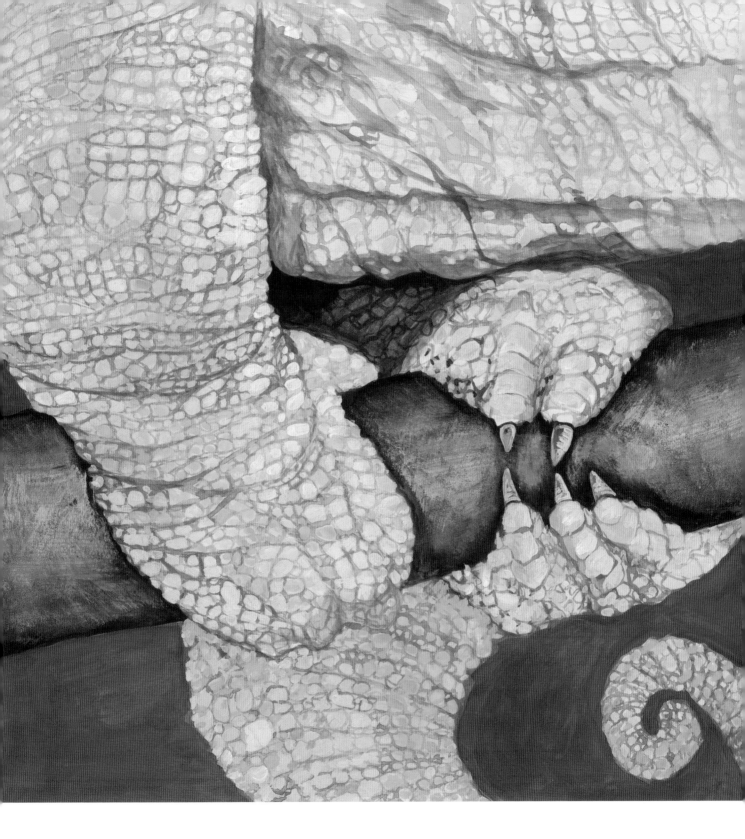

Whose toes do you suppose?

Chameleon

These toes can grip when it's tree climbing
among the leaves where this creature is hiding.
With skin changing color, it may appear to be near
then before too long seems to disappear.
Armed with eyes seeing two ways at once,
useful when there are insects to hunt.

Whose toes do you suppose?

Pangolin

Clawed toes and a body covered in scales
from the end of their nose to the tip of their tail.
A suit of armor for when danger does call,
they curl up tight and safe into a ball.
Though a scaly coat shields this unique creature,
a long, sticky tongue is their strangest feature.

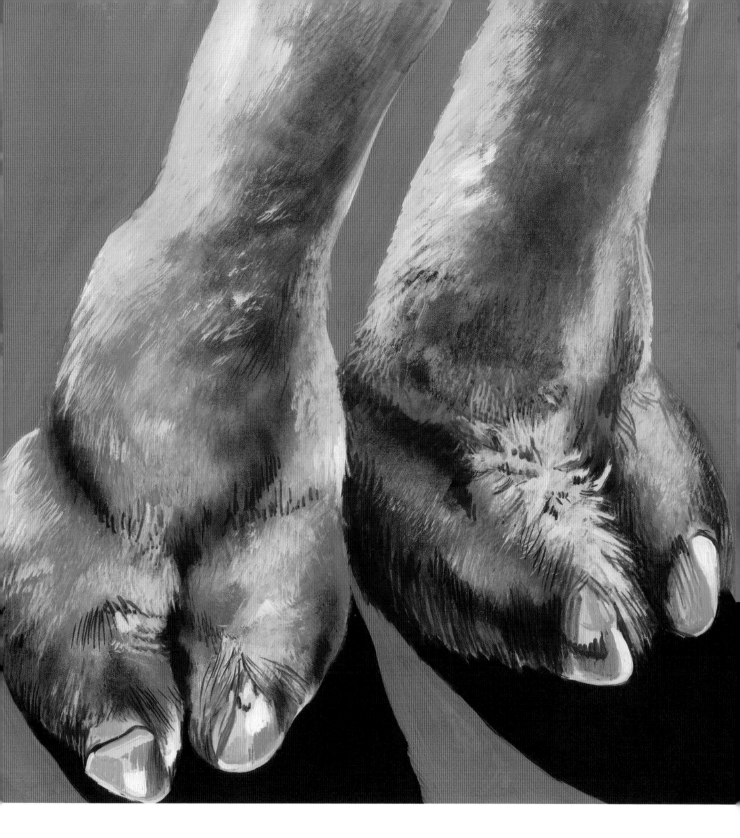

Whose toes do you suppose?

Camel

These four feet have specially designed toes
for walking on sand where not many dare go.
Two rows of eyelashes and three eyelids for each eye
are needed in deserts dusty and dry.
But a hump is their key to life under the sun.
Some have two, others just one.

Whose toes do you suppose?

Pelican

A bird with webbing between all four toes
on feet fit for swimming and diving as they go,
scooping up water with a very large bill
to hold in their pouch a tasty meal.
Giant wings spread wide to soar with ease
over rivers, lakes, and deep blue seas.

Whose toes do you suppose?

Gorilla

These amazing feet have an opposable big toe
that looks like a thumb, so even though
feet are for walking, their toes work and play.
Such intelligent creatures with skills on display,
they groom one another and at night build a nest.
They holler and hoot and pound their chest.

Whose toes do you suppose?

Kangaroo

Standing tall on large hind paws
with five curved toes and dagger-like claws.
To warn of danger, they beat the ground
like a drum, and then away they bound.
A long, strong tail and powerful stride.
In its mother's pouch, joey is safe inside.

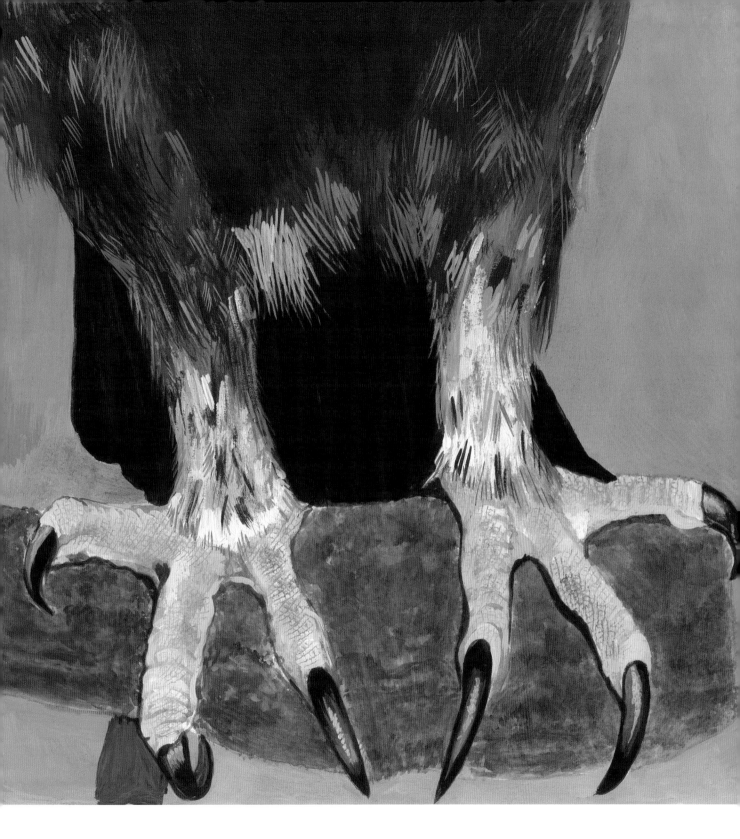

Whose toes do you suppose?

Eagle

Toes with talons have a grip like a vice.
Upon their prey they swoop, so precise.
With powerful wings and keen eyes,
in a flash, they attack by surprise.
They nest on cliffs or high in trees,
always on alert for a meal to seize.

Whose toes do you suppose?

American Coot

These toes with lobes are unusual indeed,
appearing to be larger than this creature may need.
Though such feet look strange when walking on ground,
in the water their paddling skills abound.
For this bird to get airborne can seem a tall order,
as it flaps its wings while running across water.

Whose toes do you suppose?

Gecko

These four feet have very sticky toes
that grip almost anywhere it goes.
If they lose their tail when under attack,
Amazingly, it will always grow back.
A creature without eyelids, it cannot blink.
It makes you wonder how they sleep a wink.

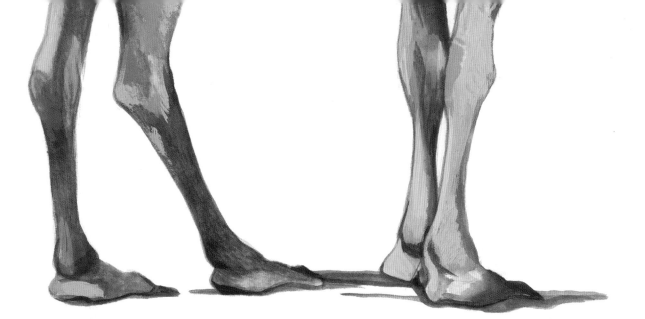

For Vin and Wendy, the outlaw in-laws. – RT

 **STARFISH BAY**
CHILDREN'S BOOKS

An imprint of Starfish Bay Publishing
www.starfishbaypublishing.com

WHOSE TOES DO YOU SUPPOSE?

Text copyright © Richard Turner, 2022
Illustrations copyright © Margaret Tolland, 2022
ISBN 978-1-76036-111-2
First Published 2022
Printed in China

Sincere thanks to Elyse Williams from Starfish Bay Children's Books for her creative efforts in preparing this edition for publication.

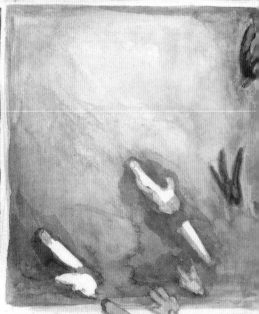